Raymond Futia

שָׁלוֹם וּבְרָכָה
Family Companion

BLACK-LINE MASTERS

by

Michelle Shapiro Abraham

Springfield, New Jersey
www.behrmanhouse.com

ISBN: 0-87441-705-8
tured in the United States of America

Dear Educator,

Family support and reinforcement are important for a Hebrew reading program to succeed. The *Shalom Uvrachah Family Companion* gives parents the tools to reinforce their child's Hebrew studies and to promote a love of Jewish learning.

The goals of the *Family Companion* are fivefold:

1. Enable parents to reinforce their child's Hebrew reading at home
2. Introduce parents who don't know Hebrew to the letters and vowels
3. Provide materials for reading practice without having to send home the textbook
4. Encourage parents to create a Hebrew-friendly environment in the home
5. Provide questions and activities for families to complete together

Contents

I FAMILY PAGES

Twenty-five double-sided Family Pages—one for each of the 25 lessons in *Shalom Uvrachah*. Each page contains:

- A listing of the new key word, letter(s), and vowel(s) taught in that lesson, with transliteration and translation
- "Now Read and Read Again"—reading drill from the student's textbook
- "Beyond the Book"—*Hebrew hints* (*bet* has a belly button), *cultural information* for the parent (why we should say 100 blessings a day!), and *activities* for the family to complete together (how to hang a mezuzah)
- Transliteration of "Now Read and Read Again"—the means for parents to follow along with their child's reading even if they themselves don't know Hebrew

II MAKE-YOUR-OWN CARDS

- The 80 Hebrew cultural words found in *Shalom Uvrachah*, laid out to fit Avery 5162 labels
- Transliteration and translation of the cultural words

How to use

1. Photocopy both sides of the Family Page as you begin each lesson in the book and send it home with your students.
2. Upon completion of the lesson, have students return the Family Page with the parent's signature, indicating that they have completed the reading practice at home.
3. If you choose, reproduce Make-Your-Own Cards on labels and attach to index cards for each child to have his or her own set of word cards. Use the word cards for review and for games such as bingo, memory, or tic-tac-toe.

With parents' reinforcement at home, in-class Hebrew reading games, and your encouragement, your students will get lots of practice for their lessons in *Shalom Uvrachah*. They will be well on their way to becoming successful Hebrew readers.

B'hatzlaḥah,

Terry Kaye

Terry Kaye

L E S S O N 1

Student's Name Raymond **Parent's Signature** Donna Kutia

NEW WORD	NEW LETTERS	NEW VOWELS
שַׁבָּת *shabat* Shabbat, rest	בּ *bet* "b" ת or תּ *tav* "t" שׁ *shin* "sh"	ַ "a" as in "father" ָ "a" as in "father"

Now Read & Read Again

1 בָּ בַּ בּ בַּ בָּ בּ

2 תָּ תַ תּ תָּ תַ ת

3 שַׁשׁ שַׁבּ שָׁת שָׁשַׁ שָׁבַּ שָׁתָּ

4 בַּשׁ תָּשׁ בַּת שַׁתּ בָּשָׁ בַּת

5 שַׁבַּשׁ תָּשַׁבּ תַּבָּשׁ תַּבַּת בַּשָׁת

6 שַׁבַּבּ בַּתָּבּ תָּתַּבּ בַּבָּת תַּבַּת

7 תַּבָּת שַׁבַּתָּ בַּשָׁת בַּשָׁשׁ בַּבָּת

8 שַׁבָּת שַׁבָּת שַׁבָּת שַׁבָּת שַׁבָּת

BEYOND THE BOOK

Learning to Read Hebrew Together

If you are not a Hebrew reader, this can be a very exciting time for you! During the next year you can learn the Hebrew letters and vowels along with your child. You can help your child practice newly acquired Hebrew reading skills and you can help create a Hebrew-friendly environment at home. Good luck, have fun, and happy learning!

"Shabbat" or "Shabbos"?

You may remember learning to say "Shabbos," instead of "Shabbat" as your child is learning. This is actually just a difference in pronunciation. Your child is learning Sephardi rather than Ashkenazi pronunciation. There are only minor differences between the two, but if you are used to the Ashkenazi pronunciation some words may sound a bit different to you. Transliteration is provided for you to check your child's pronunciation.

1 בָּ בַּ בּ בָּ בַּ בּ

b' ba ba b' ba ba

2 תָּ תַּ תּ תָּ תַּ תּ

t' ta ta t' ta ta

3 שַׁשׁ שַׁבּ שָׁת שָׁשַׁ שָׁבַּ שָׁתָּ

shata shaba shasha shat shab shash

4 בַּשׁ תָּשׁ בַּת שַׁתַּ בָּשָׁ בַּת

bat basha shata bat tash bash

5 שַׁבַּשׁ תָּשַׁבּ תַּבָּשׁ תַּבַּת בַּשָׁת

bashat tabat tabash tashab shabash

6 שַׁבַּבּ בַּתָּבּ תָּתַּבּ בַּבָּת תַּבַּת

tabat babat tatab batab shabab

7 תַּבָּת שַׁבַּתָּ בַּשָׁת בַּשָׁשׁ בַּבָּת

babat bashash bashat shabata tabat

8 שַׁבָּת שַׁבָּת שַׁבָּת שַׁבָּת שַׁבָּת

shabat shabat shabat shabat shabat

LESSON 2

Student's Name Raymond **Parent's Signature**

NEW WORD	NEW LETTER
שַׁמָשׁ *shamash* helper	מ *mem* "m"

Now Read & Read Again

1 שַׁמָ מָשׁ מַמָ מָשׁ שַׁבָּ בָּת

2 מַשׁ מַבּ מָת מַמַ מַתַּ מַבָּ

3 בַּמַ שָׁמָ תָּמָ בַּת בָּמָ תַמַ

4 מָשַׁבּ מָתַּשׁ מַבַּת מַמַת בָּמָשׁ

5 תָּמַשׁ שַׁבָּת תַּמַת מַבָּשׁ מָשַׁשׁ

6 שַׁבָּת שַׁמָשׁ מָתָּשׁ מָשַׁשׁ שַׁמָשׁ

7 שַׁמָ שַׁמָשׁ שַׁבָּ שַׁבָּת שַׁמָשׁ

8 שַׁבָּת שַׁמָשׁ שַׁבָּת שַׁמָשׁ שַׁבָּת

BEYOND THE BOOK

The Shamash Candle

The word *shamash* means "helper." It is also the name of the helper candle on the *ḥanukkiah,* the Ḥanukkah menorah. We use the *shamash* to light the other candles.

The Great Ḥanukkah Candle Debate

Our tradition teaches that there was once a great debate between Hillel and Shammai, two of our greatest ancient rabbis. Shammai believed that on the first night of Ḥanukkah we should light all eight candles, and that each night we should reduce the number of candles by one until none are left. Hillel believed that the first night we should light only one candle, adding another each night until all eight are lit. Our tradition follows Hillel, because it is said that we should always work to increase the light in the world.

- What does it mean to "increase the light in the world"?
- How can your family be a *shamash*—a helper—in increasing the light in the world?

1 שַׁמָ מָשׁ מַמָ מָשׁ שַׁבָּ בָּת

bat shaba mash mama mash shama

2 מַשׁ מַב מָת מַמַ מַתַ מַבָּ

maba mata mama mat mab mash

3 בַּמַ שָׁמָ תָּמָ בַּת בָּמָ תַּמַ

tama bama bat tama shama bama

4 מָשַׁב מָתַשׁ מַבַּת מַמַת בָּמָשׁ

bamash mamat mabat matash mashab

5 תָּמַשׁ שַׁבָּת תַּמַת מַבָּשׁ מָשַׁשׁ

mashash mabash tamat shabat tamash

6 שַׁבָּת שַׁמָשׁ מָתָשׁ מָשַׁשׁ שַׁמָשׁ

shamash mashash matash shamash shabat

7 שַׁמָ שַׁמָשׁ שַׁבָּ שַׁבָּת שַׁמָשׁ

shamash shabat shaba shamash shama

8 שַׁבָּת שַׁמָשׁ שַׁבָּת שַׁמָשׁ שַׁבָּת

shabat shamash shabat shamash shabat

LESSON 3

Student's Name ____________________ **Parent's Signature** D. Kutia

NEW WORD
כַּלָה
kalah
bride

NEW LETTERS	
ל	*lamed* "l"
כּ	*kaf* "k"
ה	*hay* "h" or silent at the end of a word

Now Read & Read Again

1 בַּ הָ תָּ הַ כַּ הָ

2 הַל הָבּ הַתּ הָשׁ הָת הַהָ

3 בָּה תָּה שַׁה לָה מַה הַה

4 תָּלָה בָּמָה לָשָׁה כַּמָה שַׁבָּת

5 לָמָה מַכָּה שָׁמָה כַּלָה לָשָׁה

6 הַבַּת הַשַׁמָשׁ הַשַׁבָּת הַמָשָׁל הַכַּלָה

7 כַּלָה הַכַּלָה מַכָּה כַּמָה לָמָה לָשָׁה

8 שַׁבָּת הַכַּלָה שַׁבָּת הַכַּלָה שַׁבָּת הַכַּלָה

BEYOND THE BOOK

The Sabbath Bride

Our tradition teaches that Shabbat is like a *kalah*—a bride. We sing a joyful song on Friday night, Lechah Dodi, in which we welcome Shabbat, the "Sabbath bride." In class your child is exploring how Shabbat is like a bride and how she comes to "visit" us each week.

Making Shabbat a Wedding Celebration

Since our tradition teaches that Shabbat is like a bride, you have a wonderful opportunity to turn your Shabbat observance into a mini-wedding celebration. Discuss with your children what you can do on a Friday night to make your own Shabbat celebration special. If your children have attended a wedding, ask them to recall the special things that happened during the reception. Were there flowers on the table? beautiful place cards? a special table setting? music or singing in the background? All of these items can enhance your Shabbat meal as you welcome the Sabbath bride.

1 בַּ הָ תָּ הַ כַּ הָ
ha ka ha ta ha ba

2 הַל הָב הַת הָשׁ הָת הַהָ
haha hat hash hat hab hal

3 בָּה תָּה שָׁה לָה מַה הַה
hah mah lah shah tah bah

4 תָּלָה בָּמָה לָשָׁה כַּמָּה שַׁבָּת
shabat kamah lashah bamah talah

5 לָמָה מַכָּה שָׁמָה כַּלָּה לָשָׁה
lashah kalah shamah makah lamah

6 הַבַּת הַשָּׁמָשׁ הַשַּׁבָּת הַמָּשָׁל הַכַּלָּה
hakalah hamashal hashabat hashamash habat

7 כַּלָּה הַכַּלָּה מַכָּה כַּמָּה לָמָה לָשָׁה
lashah lamah kamah makah hakalah kalah

8 שַׁבָּת הַכַּלָּה שַׁבָּת הַכַּלָּה שַׁבָּת הַכַּלָּה
hakalah shabat hakalah shabat hakalah shabat

L E S S O N 4

Student's Name ____________________ **Parent's Signature** ____________________

NEW WORD	NEW LETTERS	NEW VOWEL
בְּרָכָה *b'rachah* blessing	ר *resh* "r" כ *chaf* "ch" as in "Bach"	ְ *sh'va* silent or "uh" as in the sound after the "y" in "y'all"

Now Read & Read Again

1 מָכַ בָּכָ כָּכָ רָכַ תָּכָ לְכָ

2 כָה מָכַ כָּכָ כַבָּ כַּת כַשְׁ

3 רַכְ כָּמְ שַׁכְ כַּר תַּכַ בַּר

4 בָּכָה כָּכָה רַכָּה מָכַר שָׁכַר כַּלַת

5 כַּלָה כָּהָה כַּמָה מַכָּה רָכַשׁ לַכַּת

6 בָּכַת כָּכַת כָּרָה לְכָה תָּכָה לָכַשׁ

7 בָּכְתָה הַתָּכָה כָּרַכְתָּ מָכְרָה הָלַכְתָּ

8 הָלַכְתָּ בְּרָכָה בְּרָכָה הָלְכָה מָשְׁכָה

BEYOND THE BOOK

The Letter ה

New Hebrew readers often have a difficult time with the letter ה. Remind your child that it acts just like the letter "h" in English. If the letter "h" is at the beginning of a word (like "help") it makes a sound. If it is at the end of a word (like "shah") it is silent. The silent ה occurs frequently in Hebrew. Your child will get used to it with practice!

One Hundred Brachot a Day

Our tradition teaches that we should strive to say one hundred *b'rachot* (blessings) a day. There are blessings for everything, from seeing a rainbow to wearing a new jacket to eating a fruit for the first time in a season. They all begin with the *b'rachah* "formula": *Blessed are You, Adonai our God, Ruler of the Universe*… Over the next few days, help your child find things in the world for which to thank God. Use the *b'rachah* formula and add your own ending. For example, perhaps you can say a blessing during a happy family moment or upon seeing a beautiful tree. Help your child find the work of God in the wonderful world that surrounds us!

1 מָכַ בָּכָ כָּכָ רָכַ תָּכָ לְכָ
l'cha tacha racha kacha bacha macha

2 כָּה מָכַ כָּכָ כַבָּ כַּת כַשְׁ
chash kat chaba kacha macha chah

3 רַכְ כָּמְ שַׁכְ כַּר תַּכַ בַּר
bar tacha kar shach kam rach

4 בָּכָה כָּכָה רַכָּה מָכַר שָׁכַר כַּלַת
kalat shachar machar rakah kachah bachah

5 כַּלָה כָּהָה כַּמָה מַכָּה רָכַשׁ לַכַּת
lakat rachash makah kamah kahah kalah

6 בָּכַת כָּכַת כָּרָה לְכָה תָּכָה לָכַשׁ
lachash tachah l'chah karah kachat bachat

7 בָּכְתָה הַתָּכָה כָּרַכְתָּ מָכְרָה הָלַכְתָּ
halachta machrah karachta hatachah bachtah

8 הָלַכְתָּ בְּרָכָה בְּרָכָה הָלְכָה מָשְׁכָה
mashchah halchah b'rachah b'rachah halachta

LESSON 5

Student's Name ____________________ **Parent's Signature** ____________________

NEW WORD	NEW LETTERS	NEW VOWEL
הַבְדָלָה *havdalah* separation	ב *vet* "v" ד *dalet* "d"	ֲ "a" as in "father"

Now Read & Read Again

1 דָד דָר בַּד בַּר דָשׁ רָשׁ

2 דָשׁ דַת דַל דָה דָר דָב

3 מַד כַּד בַּדָ שַׁדָ הַד רַד

4 דָלָה דָבָר דְבַשׁ לָמַד הָדָר דָרָה

5 לְבַד דָהָה דָרַשׁ שָׁדַד דָשָׁה מָדַד

6 הֲבָרָה הֲדָרָה הֲלָכָה דְמָמָה הֲמָרָה

7 כָּתְבָה לָבַשְׁתָּ לָמְדָה דָרַכְתָּ מָדְדָה

8 הַבְדָלָה דְרָשָׁה הֲלָכָה בְּרָכָה הַבְדָלָה

BEYOND THE BOOK

Hebrew Hints to Help Your Child's Reading

New Hebrew readers often find it hard to distinguish between look-alike letters. In Hebrew, two letters can look the same except for a dot in the middle, for example, ב and בּ. This dot can change the sound of the letter. Or, the letters can look similar, like ר and ד, but make different sounds. Here are some Hebrew hints to help your child (and you!) memorize the sounds of the letters. As you progress, you can have fun making up your own mnemonics.

בּ	*bet*	has a "belly button"
ת	*tav*	has a "tiny toe"
מ	*mem*	has a "man on the mountain"
ד	*dalet*	looks like a "doorway"
ל	*lamed*	is "long"
ר	*resh*	is "rounded"
ב	*vet*	is "vacant"
כּ	*kaf*	has a "cough drop"

1 דָד דָר בַּדָ בַּר דָשׁ רָשׁ

dad dar bada bar dash rash

2 דָשׁ דַת דַל דָה דָר דָב

dash dat dal dah dar dav

3 מַד כַּד בַּדָ שַׁדָ הַד רַד

mad kad bada shada had rad

4 דָלָה דָבָר דְבַשׁ לָמַד הָדָר דָרָה

dalah davar d'vash lamad hadar darah

5 לְבַד דָהָה דָרַשׁ שָׁדַד דָשָׁה מָדַד

l'vad dahah darash shadad dashah madad

6 הֲמָרָה דְמָמָה הֲלָכָה הֲדָרָה הֲבָרָה

hamarah d'mamah halachah hadarah havarah

7 כָּתְבָה לָבַשְׁתָּ לָמְדָה דָרַכְתָּ מָדְדָה

katvah lavashta lamdah darachta ma'd'dah

8 הַבְדָלָה דְרָשָׁה הֲלָכָה בְּרָכָה הַבְדָלָה

havdalah d'rashah halachah b'rachah havdalah

L E S S O N 6

Student's Name ____________________ **Parent's Signature** ____________________

NEW WORD
וְאָהַבְתָּ
v'ahavta
and you shall love

NEW LETTERS	
א	*alef* no sound
ו	*vav* "v"

Now Read & Read Again

1 דָוַ שָׁוָ תָּוָ שְׁוָ וָלָ וְהָ

2 וָו וָה וַת וַר וַדָ וָאָ

3 לָוָ מַוָ כְּוַ הָוָ תָּו בַּוְ

4 דָוַר שָׁוָה תָּוָה אַוָה לָו אָבָה

5 אֲתַר דָוָה הָוָה שְׁוָא וָלָד דְבַשׁ

6 אֲשָׁרָה אַדְוָה רַאֲוָה וְאַתָּה וְאָהַב

7 אָבְדָה שַׁלְוָה וְאָכַל מְלַוָה הַדָבָר

8 וְהָלַכְתָּ וְאָהַבְתָּ וְאָמַרְתָּ וְלָמַדְתָּ וְאָהַבְתָּ

BEYOND THE BOOK

Sssh!

There are two letters in the Hebrew alphabet that have no sound. This week, your child is learning the first one—*alef* (א). (The second one is *ayin.*) If your child has difficulty with this concept, you can explain that the *alef* takes the sound of the vowel under it or after it. Occasionally, you will see a "silent" letter *with no vowel* at the end of a word. In this case, remind your child not to pronounce the letter.

"And You Shall Write it on the Doorposts of Your House"

In Deuteronomy we find the beginning of the prayer that is commonly called the V'ahavta. This prayer is part of our daily service and is also written on the parchment found in the mezuzah—which can be affixed to any doorway in your home (except the bathroom). When you affix the mezuzah say the following blessing:

Baruch atah, Adonai Eloheinu, melech ha'olam, asher kid'shanu b'mitzvotav v'tzivanu likbo'a m'zuzah.

Blessed are You, Adonai our God, Ruler of the universe, who makes us holy with commandments and commands us to affix the mezuzah.

1 דָוַ שָׁוָ תָּוָ שְׁוָ וָלָ וְהָ

v'ha vala sh'va tava shava dava

2 וָו וָה וַת וַר וָדָ וָאָ

va'a vada var vat vah vav

3 לָוָ מַוָ כְּוַ הָוָ תָּו בַּוְ

bav tav hava k'va mava lava

4 דָוַר שָׁוָה תָּוָה אַוָה לָו אָבָה

avah lav avah tavah shavah davar

5 אֲתַר דָוָה הָוָה שְׁוָא וָלָד דְּבַשׁ

d'vash valad sh'va havah davah atar

6 אֲשָׁרָה אַדְוָה רַאֲוָה וְאַתָּה וְאָהַב

v'ahav v'atah ra'avah advah asharah

7 אָבְדָה שַׁלְוָה וְאָכַל מְלַוָה הַדָבָר

hadavar m'lavah v'achal shalvah avdah

8 וְהָלַכְתָּ וְאָהַבְתָּ וְאָמַרְתָּ וְלָמַדְתָּ וְאָהַבְתָּ

v'ahavta v'lamad'ta v'amarta v'ahavta v'halachta

LESSON 7

Student's Name ____________________ **Parent's Signature** ____________________

NEW WORD
צְדָקָה
tz'dakah
tzedakah, justice

NEW LETTERS	
ק	*koof* "k"
צ	*tzadee* "tz" as in "waltz"

Now Read & Read Again

1 צַו צָב צַר צַד צָה צָל

2 כְּצַ בָּצַ אָצָ מַצָ קָצַ רָצָ

3 אָכָה צָדַק כְּצַד בָּצַר אָצָה צָרָה

4 צָבָא צָבַּר קָצַר צְבָת בָּצָל מָצָא

5 מַצָה קְצַת קַצָב מַצָב הַצָב אָצַר

6 מָצָא צָלָה צָמַד מַצָה אָצְתָּ צָמָא

7 וְרָצָה וְאָצַר צָרַמְתְּ צַוָאר צָוְאָה

8 צְדָקָה בָּצַרְתָּ מָצָאתָ צָדַקְתָּ צְדָקָה

BEYOND THE BOOK

Tzedakah

The word tzedakah comes from the Hebrew root meaning "justice." It reminds us of our obligation to make the world a better place. Maimonides defines eight levels in his Ladder of Tzedakah. The lowest level is giving begrudgingly. The highest level is giving a person a job or entering into a business partnership with a person so that he or she will no longer need to receive tzedakah.

Giving Tzedakah: Starting a Family Tradition

To teach your children about their role in making the world a better place, create a weekly ritual of giving tzedakah. You can make your own tzedakah box or buy one at your local Judaica store or synagogue gift shop. Many families give tzedakah before the lighting of the Shabbat candles. Each month your family can decide where the family tzedakah should go. This is a good opportunity to talk about the values your family considers important. Your rabbi, educator, or other congregational leader may be able to give you suggestions on where to send tzedakah.

1 צַו צָב צַר צַד צָה צָל

tzav tzav tzar tzad tzah tzal

2 כְּצַ בָּצַ אָצָ מַצָ קָצַ רָצָ

k'tza batza atza matza katza ratza

3 אָכָה צָדַק כְּצַד בָּצַר אָצָה צָרָה

achah tzadak k'tzad batzar atzah tzarah

4 צָבָא צָבַּר קָצַר צְבָת בָּצָל מָצָא

tzava tzabar katzar tz'vat batzal matza

5 מַצָה קְצַת קַצָב מַצָב הַצָב אָצַר

matzah k'tzat katzav matzav hatzav atzar

6 מָצָא צָלָה צָמַד מַצָה אָצְתָ צָמָא

matza tzalah tzamad matzah atzta tzama

7 וְרָצָה וְאָצַר צָרַמְתְ צַוָאר צָוְאָה

v'ratzah v'atzar tzaramt tzavar tzav'ah

8 צְדָקָה בָּצַרְתָ מָצָאתָ צָדַקְתָ צְדָקָה

tz'dakah batzarta matzata tzadakta tz'dakah

LESSON 8

Student's Name ____________________ **Parent's Signature** ____________________

NEW WORD
מִצְוָה
mitzvah
commandment

NEW VOWEL	
ִ	short "i" as in "bit"
ִי	"ee" as in "sheep"

Now Read & Read Again

1 מִקְ צַדִי לְבִי אֲוִי דָוִ בְּרִי

2 שִׁשָׁה הִכָּה בִּיב שְׁמִי צִיר הֲכִי

3 הִיא אִישׁ אִשָׁה אִמָא בְּכִי בְּלִי

4 רַבִּי אֲוִיר דָוִד בִּימָה דָתִי תִּיק

5 שִׁירָה תִּירָא רִמָה קְרִיאַת לְבִיבָה קָצִיר

6 צַדִיק בְּרִיאַת קַדִישׁ אָבִיב קְהִילָה מִקְרָא

7 צִיצִית בְּרִית מִילָה תִּקְוָה הַתִּקְוָה

8 מִצְוָה הַמִצְוָה בַּר מִצְוָה בַּת מִצְוָה

One Mitzvah Leads to Another

In Pirke Avot 4.2 (Ethics of the Fathers) we find the following teaching about mitzvot:

> *Ben Azai teaches: Be as quick to obey a minor mitzvah as a major one…for fulfilling one mitzvah leads to fulfilling another.*

Mitzvah Stars

Our tradition teaches that one good choice leads to more good choices. Now is the time to put your child's good choices in a Jewish context. When your child is kind to others, helps those in need, or shows respect to elders, he or she is fulfilling mitzvot (commandments in the Torah). By defining these acts as "mitzvot," you help your child see the world through Jewish eyes. At bedtime ask your child to tell you about a mitzvah he or she performed that day. Acknowledge your child's kind deeds with a reinforcing technique. For example, affix a glow-in-the-dark star to the bedroom ceiling for each mitzvah performed. Together, you can fill the world with light.

1 מִק צַדִי לְבִי אֲוִי דָוִ בְּרִי

b'ree davi avee l'vee tzadee mik

2 שִׁשָּׁה הִכָּה בִּיב שְׁמִי צִיר הֲכִי

hachee tzeer sh'mee beev hikah shishah

3 הִיא אִישׁ אִשָּׁה אִמָּא בְּכִי בְּלִי

b'lee b'chee ima ishah eesh hee

4 רַבִּי אֲוִיר דָּוִד בִּימָה דָּתִי תִּיק

teek datee beemah david aveer rabee

5 שִׁירָה תִּירָא רִמָּה קְרִיאַת לְבִיבָה קָצִיר

katzeer l'veevah k'ree'at rimah teera sheerah

6 צַדִּיק בְּרִיאַת קַדִּישׁ אָבִיב קְהִילָּה מִקְרָא

mikra k'heelah aveev kadeesh b'ree'at tzadeek

7 צִיצִית בְּרִית מִילָה תִּקְוָה הַתִּקְוָה

hatikvah tikvah meelah breet tzeetzeet

8 מִצְוָה הַמִּצְוָה בַּר מִצְוָה בַּת מִצְוָה

mitzvah bat mitzvah bar hamitzvah mitzvah

LESSON 9

Student's Name ____________________ **Parent's Signature** ____________________

NEW WORD	NEW LETTER
שְׁמַע *sh'ma* hear	ע *ayin* no sound

Now Read & Read Again

1 עָשִׂי עָתִי עָבַ צָעִי מַע דַעַ

2 עַל עָבָ עַד רַע עִיר עַר

3 וַעַד דַּעַת עַתָּה רַעַשׁ בַּעַל עָבַר

4 שְׁמַע רָעָב צָעִיר תָּקַע עִמָּה שָׁעָה

5 רָקִיעַ עָתִיד עָשִׁיר אַרְבַּע עָתִיק עִבְרִי

6 עִבְרִית מַעֲרִיב תְּקִיעָה עֲמִידָה קְעָרָה

7 שַׁעֲוָה עָבַדְתִּי שִׁבְעָה עֲתִיקָה עֲמִידָה

8 שְׁמַע תִּשְׁמַע שְׁמִיעָה קְרִיאַת שְׁמַע

BEYOND THE BOOK

Sssh!

Like the letter *alef* (א) that your child learned a few weeks ago, the letter *ayin* (ע) does not have a sound. Both letters take the sound of the vowel under or next to them. Occasionally, you will see a "silent" letter *with no vowel* at the end of a word. In this case, remind your child not to pronounce the letter.

To Be a Witness

When we see the Sh'ma prayer in its source—the Torah—we notice something very interesting. The last letter of the word *sh'ma*, ע, and the last letter of the word *eḥad*, ד, are written larger than all of the other letters.

שמע ישראל, יי אלהינו, יי אחד

Sh'ma yisrael, Adonai Eloheinu, Adonai eḥad
Hear O Israel, Adonai is our God, Adonai is One

These two letters together (עֵד) mean "witness." Our tradition teaches that one of the lessons of the Sh'ma is that each Jew is a witness that God is One.

1 עָשִׂי עָתִי עָבַ צָעִי מַע דַע
da'a ma tza'ee ava atee ashee

2 עַל עָבָ עַד רַע עִיר עַר
ar eer ra ad ava al

3 וַעַד דַעַת עַתָּה רַעַשׁ בַּעַל עָבַר
avar ba'al ra'ash atah da'at va'ad

4 שְׁמַע רָעָב צָעִיר תָּקַע עִמָּה שָׁעָה
sha'ah imah taka tza'eer ra'av sh'ma

5 רָקִיעַ עָתִיד עָשִׂיר אַרְבַּע עָתִיק עִבְרִי
ivree ateek arba asheer ateed rakee'a

6 עִבְרִית מַעֲרִיב תְּקִיעָה עֲמִידָה קְעָרָה
k'arah ameedah t'kee'ah ma'areev ivreet

7 שַׁעֲוָה עָבַדְתִּי שִׁבְעָה עֲתִיקָה עֲמִידָה
ameedah ateekah shiv'ah avad'tee sha'avah

8 שְׁמַע תִּשְׁמַע שְׁמִיעָה קְרִיאַת שְׁמַע
sh'ma k'ree'at sh'mee'ah tishma sh'ma

LESSON 10

Student's Name ____________________ **Parent's Signature** ____________________

NEW WORD
נָבִיא
navee
prophet

NEW LETTERS
נ *nun* "n"
ן final *nun* "n"

Now Read & Read Again

1 נָן נָו נְעִי קַן בִּין

2 נִין לָן דָן מָן שִׁין רָן

3 דִין בְּנִי עָנִי נָקִי אֲנִי נָא

4 שָׁנָה לָבָן עָנָו רִנָה עָנַד נַעַר

5 נָבִיא בִּינָה נְשָׁמָה מִשְׁנָה נְעָרָה

6 מַאֲמִין שְׁכִינָה כַּוָנָה נְעִילָה מַרְבִּין

7 רַעֲנָן מִשְׁכָּן לְהָבִין קַנְקַן לַמְדָן

8 נָבִיא מְדִינָה מַה נִשְׁתַּנָה נָבִיא

BEYOND THE BOOK

Final Letters

In Hebrew there are five "final letters." Final letters appear only at the end of a word. For example, the regular *nun* (נ) can be found at the beginning or in the middle of a word, but final *nun* (ן) will be found only at the end of a word. A final letter makes the same sound as its regular letter. As the year progresses, your child will learn the other four final letters.

Tanach

The word *Tanach*—the Jewish Bible—is an acronym for the three sections that make up the Bible:

T*orah*	"Teaching"	The Torah—also called the Five Books of Moses—contains the books of Genesis, Exodus, Leviticus, Numbers, and Deuteronomy.
N*'vee'eem*	"Prophets"	*N'vee'eem* contains 21 sections, including Joshua, Isaiah, and Jonah. The Haftarah reading in the Torah service is taken from this section of the Bible.
K*'tuveem*	"Writings"	*K'tuveem* includes 13 different books and scrolls, including Ruth, Esther, Song of Songs, and Chronicles. We read from *K'tuveem* on the festivals.

1 נָן נָו נְעִי קַן בִּין

been kan n'ee nav nan

2 נִין לָן דָן מָן שִׁין רָן

ran sheen man dan lan neen

3 דִין בְּנִי עָנִי נָקִי אֲנִי נָא

na anee nakee anee b'nee deen

4 שָׁנָה לָבָן עָנָו רִנָה עָנַד נַעַר

na'ar anad rinah anav lavan shanah

5 נָבִיא בִּינָה נְשָׁמָה מִשְׁנָה נְעָרָה

n'arah mishnah n'shamah beenah navee

6 מַאֲמִין שְׁכִינָה כַּוָנָה נְעִילָה מַרְבִּין

marbeen n'eelah kavanah sh'cheenah ma'ameen

7 רַעֲנָן מִשְׁכָּן לְהָבִין קַנְקַן לַמְדָן

lamdan kankan l'haveen mishkan ra'anan

8 נָבִיא מְדִינָה מַה נִשְׁתַּנָה נָבִיא

navee nishtanah mah m'deenah navee

LESSON 11

Student's Name ____________________ **Parent's Signature** ____________________

NEW WORD	NEW LETTER
חַלָה *ḥalah* ḥallah, braided bread	ח *ḥet* "ḥ" as in "Bach"

Now Read & Read Again

1 חִכָּ חָבִי חָתָ בָּח אַח צָח

2 חָל חִיל חַד חָשׁ חִישׁ חִימִי

3 קַח צַח נָח לָח אָח חַוָה

4 חִכָּה שָׁכַח חָבִיב חֲבָל חָתָן לָקַח

5 חַלָה חָלִיל וְצָחַק אַחַת חָצִיר חָנָן

6 מִנְחָה חֲמִשָׁה שָׁלְחָה חִירִיק בָּחַרְתָּ

7 רַחֲמָן הָרַחֲמָן שַׁחֲרִית חֲתִימָה חֲדָשָׁה

8 הַחַלָה הַבְּרָכָה חַלָה לְשַׁבָּת הָרַחֲמָן

BEYOND THE BOOK

Making Ḥallah

Making ḥallah is a wonderful way to bring Shabbat into your home. Below is a simple ḥallah recipe you can make together.

Ḥallah Recipe

2 packages dry yeast
2½ cups warm water
¼ cup sugar
2 teaspoons salt
⅓ cup light oil
4 eggs, lightly beaten
8–9 cups flour
1 egg mixed with 1 tablespoon water
Poppy or sesame seeds (optional)

1. In a large bowl, sprinkle yeast over warm water and allow to dissolve. (The yeast activates best if 1 Tbsp of the ¼ cup of sugar is added to the warm water.) Wait 5 minutes before adding the other ingredients.
2. Add sugar, salt, and half the flour. Mix well.
3. Stir in the eggs and oil; add the remaining flour slowly.
4. Knead the dough for 10 minutes on a board sprinkled with flour. If dough is too moist, add a little more flour.
5. Put dough in a large bowl, brush with oil, cover, and let rise for 1 hour.
6. Braid dough into two loaves: Divide dough in half. Divide each half into 3 portions. Roll each portion into a smooth rope. Braid the ropes together starting from the center and working out to each end. Tuck the ends under and place on a greased baking sheet. Cover with a towel and let rise for 1 hour.
7. Brush with beaten egg and sprinkle with seeds if desired.
8. Bake in a preheated oven at 375° for 30 minutes or until golden brown.

1 חִכָּ חָבִי חָתָ בָּח אַח צָח
tzaḥ   aḥ   baḥ   ḥata   ḥavee   ḥika

2 חָל חִיל חַד חָשׁ חִישׁ חִימִי
ḥeemee   ḥeesh   ḥash   ḥad   ḥeel   ḥal

3 קַח צַח נָח לָח אָח חַוָה
ḥavah   aḥ   laḥ   naḥ   tzaḥ   kaḥ

4 חִכָּה שָׁכַח חָבִיב חֲבָל חָתָן לָקַח
lakaḥ   ḥatan   ḥaval   ḥaveev   shachaḥ   ḥikah

5 חַלָה חָלִיל וְצָחַק אַחַת חָצִיר חָנָן
ḥanan   ḥatzeer   aḥat   v'tzaḥak   ḥaleel   ḥalah

6 מִנְחָה חֲמִשָׁה שָׁלְחָה חִירִיק בָּחַרְתָּ
baḥarta   ḥeereek   shalḥah   ḥamishah   minḥah

7 רַחֲמָן הָרַחֲמָן שַׁחֲרִית חֲתִימָה חֲדָשָׁה
ḥadashah   ḥateemah   shaḥareet   haraḥaman   raḥaman

8 הַחַלָה הַבְּרָכָה חַלָה לְשַׁבָּת הָרַחֲמָן
haraḥaman   l'shabat   ḥalah   hab'rachah   haḥalah

LESSON 12

Student's Name ____________________ **Parent's Signature** ____________________

NEW WORD	NEW LETTER
עֲלִיָה *aliyah* going up	י *yud* "y"

Now Read & Read Again

1 יָד יְהִי יַיִן יַמִי יָדִי יָמָה

2 שַׁיִשׁ יָשָׁן מִיָד נְיָר לַיִל הֲיִי

3 בַּיִת יָשָׁר יַעַר חַיָה עַיִן יָשַׁב

4 יָדַע אַיִל חַיָב יָחִיד יָקָר מַעְיָן

5 יְצִיר הָיָה יָוָן חַיִל יָצָא עֲדַיִן

6 יַחְדָו יִרְאָה יִצְחָק יַבָּשָׁה צִיַרְתִּי

7 עֲלִיָה כְּוִיָה יִוָכַח יַלְדָה יְדִיעָה

8 יְשִׁיבָה יִשְׁתַּבַּח הָיְתָה מִנְיָן עֲלִיָה

BEYOND THE BOOK

Sweet as Candy

In the synagogue, the honor of being called up to the Torah is known as an "aliyah." The Torah service is the highlight of our worship service. Our tradition teaches that the words of Torah should be as sweet as honey to our tongue. Some families give their children a piece of candy to eat at the beginning of the Torah service. What sweet associations this will promote!

1 יָד יְהִי יַיִן יַמִי יָדִי יָמָה

yad y'hee yayin yamee yadee yamah

2 שַׁיִשׁ יָשָׁן מִיָד נְיָר לַיִל הֲיִי

shayish yashan miyad n'yar layil hayee

3 בַּיִת יָשָׁר יַעַר חַיָה עַיִן יָשַׁב

bayit yashar ya'ar ḥayah ayin yashav

4 יָדַע אַיִל חַיָב יָחִיד יָקָר מַעְיָן

yada ayil ḥayav yaḥeed yakar ma'yan

5 יְצִיר הָיָה יָוָן חַיִל יָצָא עֲדַיִן

y'tzeer hayah yavan ḥayil yatza adayin

6 יַחְדָו יִרְאָה יִצְחָק יַבָּשָׁה צִיַרְתִּי

yaḥdav yir'ah yitzḥak yabashah tziyartee

7 עֲלִיָה כְּוִיָה יִוָכַח יַלְדָה יְדִיעָה

aliyah k'viyah yivachaḥ yaldah y'dee'ah

8 יְשִׁיבָה יִשְׁתַּבַּח הָיְתָה מִנְיָן עֲלִיָה

y'sheevah yishtabaḥ haytah minyan aliyah

L E S S O N 13

Student's Name ____________________ **Parent's Signature** ____________________

NEW WORD
לְחַיִּים
l'ḥayeem
to life

NEW LETTER
ם final *mem* "m"

Now Read & Read Again

1 הָלַם אַחִים עָלִים מִרְיָם בַּדִים תָּרַם

2 אִיִים שְׁנַיִם בָּתִּים אָדָם דַקִים מִצְרַיִם

3 חָכָם רַעַם יָמִים רַבִּים חַיִים דָמַם

4 בָּנִים מַיִם אָדָם שְׁתַּיִם מִלִים אָשָׁם

5 נָשִׁים שָׁמַיִם דְבָרִים יָדַיִם קָמִים עָלִים

6 אַבְרָהָם נְבִיאִים כְּרָמִים שִׁבְעִים אֲנָשִׁים

7 עִבְרִים רַחֲמִים יְלָדִים צַדִיקִים מְלָכִים

8 עֲבָדִים יְצִיאַת מִצְרַיִם לְחַיִים לְחַיִים

BEYOND THE BOOK

Final Mem

Final *mem* is the second of the five final letters. Final *mem* can appear only at the end of a word and makes the "m" sound.

Eighteen for Life?

The letters of the Hebrew *alef bet* also have numerical value. The system of explaining a word according to the numerical value of its letters is known as *gematria*. The letters *alef* through *tet* represent one through nine, *yud* has the value of ten, *chaf* is twenty, *lamed* is thirty, and so on. The word *ḥai* (חַי)—"life"—corresponds to eight plus ten, or eighteen. You may follow the tradition of giving gifts in increments of eighteen ("I gave double *ḥai*"—thirty-six dollars).

1 הָלַם אַחִים עָלִים מִרְיָם בַּדִים תָּרַם

taram badeem miryam aleem aḥeem halam

2 אִיִים שְׁנַיִם בָּתִּים אָדָם דַּקִים מִצְרַיִם

mitzrayim dakeem adam bateem sh'nayim iyeem

3 חָכָם רַעַם יָמִים רַבִּים חַיִים דָמַם

damam ḥayeem rabeem yameem ra'am ḥacham

4 בָּנִים מַיִם אָדָם שְׁתַיִם מִלִים אָשָׁם

asham mileem sh'tayeem adam mayeem baneem

5 נָשִׁים שָׁמַיִם דְבָרִים יָדַיִם קָמִים עָלִים

aleem kameem yadayim d'vareem shamayim nasheem

6 אַבְרָהָם נְבִיאִים כְּרָמִים שִׁבְעִים אֲנָשִׁים

anasheem shiv'eem k'rameem n'vee'eem avraham

7 עִבְרִים רַחֲמִים יְלָדִים צַדִיקִים מְלָכִים

m'lacheem tzadeekeem y'ladeem raḥameem ivreem

8 עֲבָדִים יְצִיאַת מִצְרַיִם לְחַיִים לְחַיִים

l'ḥayeem l'ḥayeem mitzrayim y'tzee'at avadeem

LESSON 14

Student's Name ____________________ **Parent's Signature** ____________________

NEW WORD
תּוֹרָה
torah
Torah, teaching

NEW VOWELS	
וֹ	"o" as in "wrote" (some say "aw" as in "fall")
◌ֹ	"o" as in "wrote" (some say "aw" as in "fall")

Now Read & Read Again

1 כֹל לֹא אוֹת יוֹם חוֹל צֹאן

2 עוֹד קוֹל מוֹת שׁוֹר צוֹם חוֹר

3 שָׁמֹעַ יָבֹא אֹתָם דָתוֹ אָנֹכִי כְּמוֹ

4 אָבוֹת מְאֹד כְּבוֹד לָשׁוֹן נָכוֹן שָׁעוֹת

5 קָדוֹשׁ תּוֹרָה צִיוֹן מוֹרָה תְּהֹם מְלֹא

6 שְׁלֹמֹה אַהֲרֹן יַעֲקֹב אֲדוֹן עוֹלָם

7 הַמוֹצִיא שַׁבַּת שָׁלוֹם רֹאשׁ הַשָׁנָה

8 תּוֹרָה בְּרָכוֹת מִצְווֹת דוֹרוֹת כֹּהֲנִים

BEYOND THE BOOK

Vav the Vowel

Your child has learned that the letter ו has a "v" sound. However, when the letter ו has a dot above it (וֹ) or next to it (וּ), it becomes a vowel. If the dot is above, the vowel makes the sound "oh" as in "wrote". Sometimes the dot stands by itself without the ו and still makes the "oh" sound (כֹּל).

The Torah Cycle

The Torah is divided into fifty-four portions called *parashiyot.* Each week we read the Portion of the Week—*parashat hashavua.* We begin and end the annual cycle of reading the Torah on the holiday of Simḥat Torah. Our ancient rabbis said of the Torah: "Turn it and turn it again, for everything is within it."

What do you think "turn it and turn it again" means?

1 כֹּל לֹא אוֹת יוֹם חוֹל צֹאן

kol lo ot yom ḥol tzon

2 עוֹד קוֹל מוֹת שׁוֹר צוֹם חוֹר

od kol mot shor tzom ḥor

3 שָׁמֹעַ יָבֹא אֹתָם דָתוֹ אָנֹכִי כְּמוֹ

shamo'a yavo otam dato anochee k'mo

4 אָבוֹת מְאֹד כְּבוֹד לָשׁוֹן נָכוֹן שָׁעוֹת

avot m'od k'vod lashon nachon sha'ot

5 קָדוֹשׁ תּוֹרָה צִיוֹן מוֹרָה תְּהֹם מְלֹא

kadosh torah tziyon morah t'hom m'lo

6 שְׁלֹמֹה אַהֲרֹן יַעֲקֹב אֲדוֹן עוֹלָם

sh'lomoh aharon ya'akov adon olam

7 הַמּוֹצִיא שַׁבָּת שָׁלוֹם רֹאשׁ הַשָּׁנָה

hamotzee shabat shalom rosh hashanah

8 תּוֹרָה בְּרָכוֹת מִצְווֹת דוֹרוֹת כֹּהֲנִים

torah b'rachot mitzvot dorot kohaneem

LESSON 15

Student's Name ____________________ **Parent's Signature** ____________________

NEW WORD
טַלִית
taleet
tallit, prayer shawl

NEW LETTER
ט *tet* "t"

Now Read & Read Again

1 טוֹן טִיב מָט אַט חַיָט מוֹטוֹ

2 טוֹב טַל אִטִי טָרִי שׁוֹט קָט

3 מִטָה מוֹט קָטָן חִטָה שָׁחַט לָטַשׁ

4 לְאַט מָטָר חָטָא מְעַט שְׁבָט בָּטַח

5 טַלִית טָהוֹר אָטָד טַעם טִבְעִי טָמַן

6 קְטַנָה עֲטָרָה מִקְלָט חֲטָאִים הִבִּיטָה

7 שְׁבָטִים טוֹבִים בִּטָחוֹן נְטִילַת יָדַיִם

8 טַלִית שָׁנָה טוֹבָה יוֹם טוֹב

BEYOND THE BOOK

Getting Ready to Pray

A tallit is the prayer shawl that many Jewish adults wear when they pray. There are ways we can prepare to pray or to study Torah. For example, we can put on a tallit and kippah, dress in neat clothing, say a blessing, or even meditate silently. When you and your family go to synagogue, think of ways you can prepare to pray. Perhaps you can share something good that happened during the week, or tell of something you hope to do better in the week to come. You may want to describe something special you saw in nature or say a kind word about each family member. Perhaps you can just enjoy a quiet family moment together!

1 טוֹן טִיב מָט אַט חַיָּט מוֹטוֹ

moto ḥayat at mat teev ton

2 טוֹב טַל אִטִי טָרִי שׁוֹט קָט

kat shot taree itee tal tov

3 מִטָה מוֹט קָטָן חִטָה שָׁחַט לָטַשׁ

latash shaḥat ḥitah katan mot mitah

4 לְאַט מָטָר חָטָא מְעַט שְׁבָט בָּטַח

bataḥ sh'vat m'at ḥata matar l'at

5 טַלִית טָהוֹר אָטָד טַעַם טִבְעִי טָמַן

taman tiv'ee ta'am atad tahor taleet

6 קְטַנָה עֲטָרָה מִקְלָט חֲטָאִים הִבִּיטָה

hibeetah ḥata'eem miklat atarah k'tanah

7 שְׁבָטִים טוֹבִים בִּטָחוֹן נְטִילַת יָדַיִם

yadayim n'teelat bitaḥon toveem sh'vateem

8 טַלִית שָׁנָה טוֹבָה יוֹם טוֹב

tov yom tovah shanah taleet

LESSON 16

Student's Name ____________________ **Parent's Signature** ____________________

NEW WORD
אֱמֶת
emet
truth

NEW VOWELS	
◌ֶ	"e" as in "set"
◌ֱ	"e" as in "set"

Now Read & Read Again

1 אֶת אֶל שֶׁלִי שֶׁלֹא אֱמֶת אַתֶּן

2 אֲשֶׁר שֶׁמֶשׁ יֶלֶד לָכֶם אֹהֶל אֶבֶן

3 אַתֶּם נֶצַח חֹדֶשׁ כֹּתֶל טֶרֶם אֶחָד

4 רוֹצֶה שֶׁבַע עֶרֶב מוֹרֶה נֶאֱמָן יִהְיֶה

5 וְנֶאֱמַר מְחַיֶּה רוֹעֶה עוֹלֶה הֶחֱלִיט שְׁמוֹנֶה

6 לְעוֹלָם וָעֶד תּוֹרַת אֱמֶת מְצַוֶּה אֶתְכֶם

7 אֲרוֹן הַקֹּדֶשׁ כֶּתֶר תּוֹרָה וַיֹּאמֶר אֱלֹהִים

8 אֱלֹהִים הַמּוֹצִיא לֶחֶם אֱמֶת וָצֶדֶק

BEYOND THE BOOK

The Struggle to Tell the Truth

Discuss with your child this saying: "Truth is its own reward." Why is it important to tell the truth? Can you think of times when it was difficult to tell the truth? Whom do we hurt when we do not tell the truth? Why do you think that Judaism would make it a virtue to tell the truth?

1 אֶת אֶל שֶׁלִּי שֶׁלֹּא אֱמֶת אַתֶּן

aten emet shelo shelee el et

2 אֲשֶׁר שֶׁמֶשׁ יֶלֶד לָכֶם אֹהֶל אֶבֶן

even ohel lachem yeled shemesh asher

3 אַתֶּם נֶצַח חֹדֶשׁ כֹּתֶל טֶרֶם אֶחָד

eḥad terem kotel ḥodesh netzaḥ atem

4 רוֹצֶה שֶׁבַע עֶרֶב מוֹרֶה נֶאֱמָן יִהְיֶה

yih'yeh ne'eman moreh erev sheva rotzeh

5 וְנֶאֱמַר מְחַיֶּה רוֹעֶה עוֹלֶה הֶחֱלִיט שְׁמוֹנֶה

sh'moneh heḥeleet oleh ro'eh m'ḥayeh v'ne'emar

6 לְעוֹלָם וָעֶד תּוֹרַת אֱמֶת מְצַוֶּה אֶתְכֶם

etchem m'tzaveh emet torat va'ed l'olam

7 אֲרוֹן הַקֹּדֶשׁ כֶּתֶר תּוֹרָה וַיֹּאמֶר אֱלֹהִים

eloheem vayomer torah keter hakodesh aron

8 אֱלֹהִים הַמּוֹצִיא לֶחֶם אֱמֶת וָצֶדֶק

vatzedek emet leḥem hamotzee eloheem

LESSON 17

Student's Name ______________________ **Parent's Signature** ______________________

NEW WORD
פֶּסַח
pesaḥ
Passover

NEW LETTERS	
פּ	*pay* "p"
ס	*samech* "s"

Now Read & Read Again

1 כּוֹס סֶלַע מַס פֶּסַח סְתָו סִיוָן

2 סְתָם חֶסֶד סַבָּא סַבְתָּא חָסִיד כַּסְפּוֹ

3 נִיסָן סִדְרָה חַסְדּוֹ סַנְדָּק יְסוֹד מִסְפָּר

4 מָסֹרֶת נִסִּים נִכְנָס כְּסוֹד מְנַסֶּה לַעֲסֹק

5 סְבִיבוֹן מְסָבִיב בָּסִיס הִסְפִּיד וְנִסְכּוֹ מַחְסִי

6 מְסַפֶּרֶת כְּנֶסֶת נִסְפָּח הַכְנָסַת מַסְפִּיק

7 חֲסָדִים חֲסִידִים פַּרְנָסָה סְלִיחָה סְלִיחוֹת

8 פֶּסַח כַּרְפַּס חֲרוֹסֶת מַצָּה מָרוֹר פֶּסַח

BEYOND THE BOOK

Bring Passover into Your Home

Passover is a home-based holiday. When we bring Passover into our homes, we fulfill the commandment "You shall personally remember when you went out from the land of Egypt." Here are a few ideas for fun home observance:

- Have your children make stick puppets for the major characters in the Passover story. At the seder, children can act out the story using their puppets.
- Decorate the house with fresh flowers, or use tissue-paper flowers that can be left up for the whole week.
- Make playful Passover foods like matzah pizza or matzah cookies. You can find terrific children's Passover cookbooks at your local Judaica store or synagogue gift shop.
- Your child is almost a Hebrew reader! Choose a few words or sentences in the Hagaddah and have your child read for the family in Hebrew.

1 כּוֹס סֶלַע מַס פֶּסַח סְתָו סִיוָן

seevan stav pesaḥ mas sela kos

2 סְתָם חֶסֶד סַבָּא סַבְתָּא חָסִיד כַּסְפּוֹ

kaspo ḥaseed savta saba ḥesed stam

3 נִיסָן סִדְרָה חַסְדּוֹ סַנְדָּק יְסוֹד מִסְפָּר

mispar y'sod sandak ḥasdo sidrah neesan

4 מָסֹרֶת נִסִּים נִכְנָס כְּסוֹד מְנַסֶּה לַעֲסֹק

la'asok m'naseh k'sod nichnas niseem masoret

5 סְבִיבוֹן מְסַבִּיב בָּסִיס הִסְפִּיד וְנִסְכּוֹ מַחְסִי

maḥsee v'nisko hispeed basees misaveev s'veevon

6 מְסַפֶּרֶת כְּנֶסֶת נִסְפָּח הַכְנָסַת מַסְפִּיק

maspeek hachnasat nispaḥ k'neset m'saperet

7 חֲסָדִים חֲסִידִים פַּרְנָסָה סְלִיחָה סְלִיחוֹת

s'leeḥot s'leeḥah parnasah ḥaseedeem ḥasadeem

8 פֶּסַח כַּרְפַּס חֲרוֹסֶת מַצָּה מָרוֹר פֶּסַח

pesaḥ maror matzah ḥaroset karpas pesaḥ

LESSON 18

Student's Name ____________________ **Parent's Signature** ____________________

NEW WORD
שׁוֹפָר
shofar
shofar, ram's horn

NEW LETTER
פ *fay* "f"

Now Read & Read Again

1 יָפֶה עָפָר כְּפִי נֶפֶשׁ חֹפֶשׁ צוֹפֶה

2 אֹפִי תָּפַס נָפַל אָפָה יָפִים נַפְשִׁי

3 אֹפֶן אֶפֶס צָפוֹן שֶׁפַע כֹּפֶר יִפְתֶּה

4 אָסַפְתָּ אֶפְשָׁר תְּפִלָּה מַפְטִיר תִּפְתַּח לִפְעָמִים

5 תְּפִלּוֹת סְפָרִים סוֹפְרִים לְפָנִים צוֹפִיָּה אַפְקִיד

6 לִפְדוֹת נוֹפְלִים טוֹטָפֹת נַפְשְׁכֶם תִּפְאֶרֶת

7 אֲפִיקוֹמָן הַפְטָרָה שׁוֹפְטִים כְּמִפְעָלוֹ תְּפִילִין

8 שׁוֹפָר תְּפִלָּה תְּפִילִין מַפְטִיר הַפְטָרָה

BEYOND THE BOOK

Hebrew Letter Hints

Your child has learned almost all of the letters in the *alef bet*! Here are some more "reading hints" to remember the names and sounds of the letters.

פּ	*pay*	has a "polka dot"
ה	*hay*	is a "house" with a "hole"
ט	*tet*	is open on the "top"
ס	*samech*	is a "slippery circle"

1 יָפֶה עָפָר כְּפִי נֶפֶשׁ חֹפֶשׁ צוֹפֶה

tzofeh hofesh nefesh k'fee afar yafeh

2 אֹפִי תָּפַס נָפַל אָפָה יָפִים נַפְשִׁי

nafshee yafeem afah nafal tafas ofee

3 אֹפֶן אֶפֶס צָפוֹן שֶׁפַע כֹּפֶר יִפְתֶּה

yifteh kofer shefa tzafon efes ofen

4 אָסַפְתָּ אֶפְשָׁר תְּפִלָּה מַפְטִיר תִּפְתַּח לִפְעָמִים

lif'ameem tiftah mafteer t'filah efshar asafta

5 תְּפִלּוֹת סְפָרִים סוֹפְרִים לְפָנִים צוֹפִיָּה אַפְקִיד

afkeed tzofiyah l'faneem sofreem s'fareem t'filot

6 לִפְדּוֹת נוֹפְלִים טוֹטָפֹת נַפְשְׁכֶם תִּפְאֶרֶת

tif'eret nafsh'chem totafot nofleem lifdot

7 אֲפִיקוֹמָן הַפְטָרָה שׁוֹפְטִים כְּמִפְעָלוֹ תְּפִלִּין

t'feeleen k'mif'alo shofteem haftarah afeekoman

8 שׁוֹפָר תְּפִלָּה תְּפִלִּין מַפְטִיר הַפְטָרָה

haftarah mafteer t'feeleen t'filah shofar

L E S S O N 19

Student's Name ____________________ **Parent's Signature** ____________________

NEW WORD	NEW LETTER	NEW VOWEL
עֵץ חַיִּים *etz ḥayeem* tree of life	ץ final *tzadee* "tz"	ֵ "e" as in "pet" (or "ei" as in "vein") ֵי "ei" as in "vein"

Now Read & Read Again

1 אֶרֶץ חָמֵץ מַצָּה חָפֵץ קַיִץ אֹמֶץ

2 קוֹץ קוֹצִים בּוֹץ פָּרַץ קוֹפֵץ קוֹפֶצֶת

3 נוֹצֵץ לוֹחֵץ צַנְחָן עָצִיץ מִיץ נִמְצַץ

4 אִמֵּץ אֶמְצַע מֶרֶץ אָמִיץ הֵצִיץ צִיֵּן

5 לִקְפֹּץ קְפִיצָה קָמַץ חוֹלֵץ חוֹלֵם הֵפִיץ

6 רוֹחֵץ רָחֲצָה יוֹעֵץ צִפֹּרֶן וֶאֱמַץ פֶּרֶץ

7 לְשַׁבֵּץ נִצְטַוָּה מֵלִיץ צְבָעִים צָפוֹן חָמִיץ

8 עֵץ חַיִּים הַמּוֹצִיא לֶחֶם מִן הָאָרֶץ

Behrman House, Inc. *Shalom Uvrachah Family Companion*

BEYOND THE BOOK

It Is a Tree of Life

Our tradition uses many different metaphors to describe the Torah. When we call the Torah a "tree of life," we are reminded that the Torah gives us life and sustains us. Read together the following teachings about the Torah. Which do you prefer? Why?

- "Even as rain gives life to the world, so words of Torah give life to the world."
- "Why is Torah likened to a fig tree? Because all other fruits contain useless matter. Dates have pits, grapes have seeds, pomegranates have rinds. But the fig, all of it, is edible. So words of Torah have no worthless matter in them."

As a family, write your own metaphor to describe the Torah.

1 אֶרֶץ חָמֵץ מַצָה חָפֵץ קַיִץ אֹמֶץ
ometz kayitz ḥafetz matzah ḥametz eretz

2 קוֹץ קוֹצִים בּוֹץ פָּרַץ קוֹפֵץ קוֹפֶצֶת
kofetzet kofetz paratz botz kotzeem kotz

3 נוֹצֵץ לוֹחֵץ צַנְחָן עָצִיץ מִיץ נִמְצַץ
nimtzatz meetz atzeetz tzanḥan loḥetz notzetz

4 אִמֵץ אֶמְצַע מֶרֶץ אָמִיץ הֵצִיץ צִיֵן
tziyen hetzeetz ameetz meretz emtza imetz

5 לִקְפֹּץ קְפִּיצָה קָמַץ חוֹלֵץ חוֹלֵם הֵפִּיץ
hefeetz ḥolem ḥoletz kamatz k'feetzah likfotz

6 רוֹחֵץ רָחֲצָה יוֹעֵץ צִפֹּרֶן וֶאֱמַץ פֶּרֶץ
peretz ve'ematz tziporen yo'etz raḥatzah roḥetz

7 לְשַׁבֵּץ נִצְטַוָּה מֵלִיץ צְבָעִים צָפוֹן חָמִיץ
ḥameetz tzafon tz'va'eem meleetz nitztavah l'shabetz

8 עֵץ חַיִּים הַמּוֹצִיא לֶחֶם מִן הָאָרֶץ
ha'aretz min leḥem hamotzee ḥayeem etz

LESSON 20

Student's Name ____________________ **Parent's Signature** ____________________

NEW WORD
יִשְׂרָאֵל
yisra'el
Israel

NEW LETTER
שׂ *sin* "s"

Now Read & Read Again

1 שֶׂה שִׂים שַׂר שָׂם שַׂק שִׂיא

2 שָׂרָה שָׂנֵא שָׂמַח עֶשֶׂר עֹשֶׂה מַשָׂא

3 שָׂרָה שָׂרָה שָׂמָה שַׂעַר שָׂשׂוֹן

4 שֵׂעָר שָׂכָר שָׂפָה יִשָׂא בָּשָׂר שֵׂכֶל

5 שָׂדֶה פָּשַׂט שֶׂבַע עֶשֶׂר עָשָׂה תַּיִשׂ

6 שִׂמְחַת תּוֹרָה שְׁמוֹנֶה עֶשְׂרֵה עֲשֶׂרֶת הַדִּבְּרוֹת

7 שְׁמַע יִשְׂרָאֵל שִׂים שָׁלוֹם עוֹשֶׂה שָׁלוֹם

8 עַם יִשְׂרָאֵל בְּנֵי יִשְׂרָאֵל אֶרֶץ יִשְׂרָאֵל

BEYOND THE BOOK

Letter Hints

The Hebrew letters שׁ and שׂ are two of the most difficult letters for new Hebrew readers because they look so alike. If the dot is on the right side of the letter, the letter makes a "sh" sound. If the dot is on the left, the letter makes a "s" sound. Perhaps you will remember the difference if you say, "A *sin* is never right," therefore if the dot is on the right, it must be a *shin*.

The Meanings of Yisra'el

The word *yisra'el* has several different meanings in our heritage. In the Torah, after our patriarch Jacob wrestled with an angel, God renamed Jacob *yisra'el,* or "the one who wrestled with God." The Jewish people were called *b'nei yisra'el*—"the children of Israel"—or *am yisra'el*—"the nation of Israel." *Eretz yisra'el* refers to the biblical "land of Israel." The modern Jewish state is called *m'dinat yisra'el*—"the State of Israel."

1 שֶׂה שִׂים שַׂר שָׂם שַׂק שִׂיא

see sak sam sar seem seh

2 שָׂרָה שָׂנֵא שָׂמַח עֶשֶׂר עֹשֶׂה מַשָּׂא

masa oseh eser samaḥ sa'ne sarah

3 שָׁרָה שָׂרָה שָׁמָה שָׂמָה שַׁעַר שָׂשׂוֹן

sason sha'ar samah shamah sarah sharah

4 שֵׂעָר שָׂכָר שָׂפָה יִשָּׂא בָּשָׂר שֵׂכֶל

sechel basar yisa safah sachar se'ar

5 שָׂדֶה פָּשַׁט שֶׁבַע עֶשֶׂר עָשָׂה תַּיִשׁ

tayish asah eser sheva pashat sadeh

6 שִׂמְחַת תּוֹרָה שְׁמוֹנֶה עֶשְׂרֵה עֲשֶׂרֶת הַדִּבְּרוֹת

hadibrot aseret esreh sh'moneh torah simḥat

7 שְׁמַע יִשְׂרָאֵל שִׂים שָׁלוֹם עוֹשֶׂה שָׁלוֹם

shalom oseh shalom seem yisra'el sh'ma

8 עַם יִשְׂרָאֵל בְּנֵי יִשְׂרָאֵל אֶרֶץ יִשְׂרָאֵל

yisra'el eretz yisra'el b'nei yisra'el am

LESSON 21

Student's Name ____________________ **Parent's Signature** ____________________

NEW WORDS
חַג שָׂמֵחַ
ḥag same'aḥ
happy holiday

NEW LETTER
ג *gimel* "g"

Now Read & Read Again

1 שָׂמֵחַ יָרֵחַ אוֹרֵחַ נָשִׂיחַ מֵנִיחַ בַּכֹּחַ

2 מָשִׁיחַ פּוֹקֵחַ סוֹלֵחַ פּוֹתֵחַ פָּתַח לִפְתֹּחַ

3 לְשַׁבֵּחַ מְנַצֵּחַ שׁוֹלֵחַ מָנוֹחַ שָׁלִיחַ מַפְתֵּחַ

4 מַצְמִיחַ מִשְׁלוֹחַ הִצְלִיחַ לוֹקֵחַ לְשַׂמֵּחַ פּוֹרֵחַ

5 מַשְׁגִּיחַ הַשְׁגָּחָה אָשִׂיחַ שִׂיחָה מְשַׂמֵּחַ שָׂמַח

6 הִבְטִיחַ בָּטַח טוֹרֵחַ טָרַח פִּקֵּחַ נִפְקַח

7 בּוֹרֵחַ לִבְרֹחַ בָּרַח לִסְלֹחַ סָלַח סְלִיחָה

8 מָשִׁיחַ חַג שָׂמֵחַ פֶּסַח הַגָּדָה מְגִלָּה

BEYOND THE BOOK

"Aḥ" at the End of a Word

Usually when we read a letter-vowel combination we pronounce the letter first and then its vowel. However, when the letter and vowel חַ appear at the *end* of a word, we read it as "aḥ" instead of "ḥa." Remember, this occurs only at the end of a word and only for this letter-vowel combination.

Ḥag Same'aḥ Cards

Making *Ḥag Same'aḥ* cards with your children can be both a creative way to reinforce their Hebrew learning and a thoughtful yet inexpensive way to send a gift to a grandparent or a family friend. Your children can make cards on the computer or by hand. Have them add the Hebrew phrase "*ḥag same'aḥ.*" *Ḥag Same'aḥ* cards can be sent for Sukkot, Pesaḥ, or Shavuot, but they are especially appropriate on Rosh Hashanah, when we wish people "*shanah tovah*" (a good year).

1 שָׂמֵחַ יָרֵחַ אוֹרֵחַ נָשִׂיחַ מֵנִיחַ בַּכֹּחַ

bako'aḥ me'nee'aḥ nasee'aḥ ore'aḥ yare'aḥ same'aḥ

2 מָשִׂיחַ פּוֹקֵחַ סוֹלֵחַ פּוֹתֵחַ פָּתַח לִפְתֹּחַ

lifto'aḥ pataḥ pote'aḥ sole'aḥ poke'aḥ mashee'aḥ

3 לְשַׁבֵּחַ מְנַצֵּחַ שׁוֹלֵחַ מָנוֹחַ שָׁלִיחַ מַפְתֵּחַ

mafte'aḥ shalee'aḥ mano'aḥ shole'aḥ m'natze'aḥ l'shabe'aḥ

4 מַצְמִיחַ מִשְׁלוֹחַ הִצְלִיחַ לוֹקֵחַ לְשַׂמֵּחַ פּוֹרֵחַ

pore'aḥ l'same'aḥ loke'aḥ hitzlee'aḥ mishlo'aḥ matzmee'aḥ

5 מַשְׂגִיחַ הַשְׂגָחָה אָשִׂיחַ שִׂיחָה מְשַׂמֵּחַ שָׂמַח

samaḥ m'same'aḥ seeḥah asee'aḥ hashgaḥah mashgee'aḥ

6 הִבְטִיחַ בָּטַח טוֹרֵחַ טָרַח פִּקֵּחַ נִפְקַח

nifkaḥ pike'aḥ taraḥ tore'aḥ bataḥ hivtee'aḥ

7 בּוֹרֵחַ לִבְרֹחַ בָּרַח לִסְלֹחַ סָלַח סְלִיחָה

s'leeḥah salaḥ lislo'aḥ baraḥ livro'aḥ bore'aḥ

8 מָשִׂיחַ חַג שָׂמֵחַ פֶּסַח הַגָּדָה מְגִלָּה

m'gilah hagadah pesaḥ same'aḥ ḥag mashee'aḥ

LESSON 22

Student's Name ____________________ **Parent's Signature** ____________________

NEW WORD
קִדּוּשׁ
kidush
Kiddush

NEW VOWELS	
וּ	"u" as in "tube"
◌ֻ	"u" as in "tube"

Now Read & Read Again

1 חֻמָּשׁ לוּחַ כֻּלָּם וְהָיוּ סֻכָּה טֹבוּ

2 עָלֵינוּ לִבֵּנוּ סֻכּוֹת שָׁבוּעַ חֲנֻכָּה קִבּוּץ

3 קִדּוּשׁ שֻׁלְחָן מְשֻׁבָּח סִדּוּר מְצֻיָּן כֻּלָּנוּ

4 הַלְלוּיָה גְּדֻלָּה פָּסוּק יְשׁוּעָה נְטוּיָה אֲנַחְנוּ

5 וּבְנֻחֹה לוּלָב וְיָפֻצוּ וַיְכֻלוּ וְיָנֻסוּ דַּיֵנוּ

6 תְּמוּנָה וְצִוָּנוּ אֵלִיָּהוּ הַנָּבִיא בָּרְכוּ קֻשְׁיוֹת

7 קְדֻשָּׁה יְהוּדִים פּוּרִים יוֹם כִּפּוּר שָׁבוּעוֹת

8 יְרוּשָׁלַיִם אֱלֹהֵינוּ שֶׁהֶחֱיָנוּ אָבִינוּ מַלְכֵּנוּ

BEYOND THE BOOK

"Oh" and "Ooh"

The vowels וֹ and וּ are both built on the letter *vav*. If your child is having difficulty telling the two letters apart, give him or her this helpful Hebrew hint:

וֹ The dot is "oh"-ver the letter.

וּ The dot is in the letter's stomach and it says "ooh."

Holding Your Kiddush Cup

The simple act of holding a Kiddush cup can teach us a lesson! Usually, we hold a cup by putting our hand around it. Some people, however, hold their Kiddush cup by balancing the cup on the palm of their hand and bringing their fingers around the base to secure it. What does this teach us? During the week we seem to face the world with our knuckles out, protecting ourselves and closing ourselves off from others. But on Shabbat we are reminded to face the world with our palms open to others and to the beauty of the world around us.

1 חֻמָשׁ לוּחַ כֻּלָם וְהָיוּ סֻכָּה טֹבוּ

ḥumash lu'aḥ kulam v'hayu sukah tovu

2 עָלֵינוּ לִבֵּנוּ סֻכּוֹת שָׁבוּעַ חֲנֻכָּה קִבּוּץ

aleinu libenu sukot shavu'a ḥanukah kibutz

3 קִדּוּשׁ שֻׁלְחָן מְשֻׁבָּח סִדּוּר מְצֻיָּן כֻּלָנוּ

kidush shulḥan m'shubaḥ sidur m'tzuyan kulanu

4 הַלְלוּיָה גְּדֻלָה פָּסוּק יְשׁוּעָה נְטוּיָה אֲנַחְנוּ

hal'luyah g'dulah pasuk y'shu'ah n'tuyah anaḥnu

5 וּבְנֻחֹה לוּלָב וְיָפֻצוּ וַיְכֻלוּ וְיָנֻסוּ דַּיֵנוּ

uv'nuḥoh lulav v'yafutzu va'y'chulu v'yanusu dayenu

6 תְּמוּנָה וְצִוָּנוּ אֵלִיָּהוּ הַנָּבִיא בָּרְכוּ קֻשְׁיוֹת

t'munah v'tzivanu eliyahu hanavee bar'chu kushiyot

7 קְדֻשָׁה יְהוּדִים פּוּרִים יוֹם כִּפּוּר שָׁבוּעוֹת

k'dushah y'hudeem pureem yom kipur shavu'ot

8 יְרוּשָׁלַיִם אֱלֹהֵינוּ שֶׁהֶחֱיָנוּ אָבִינוּ מַלְכֵּנוּ

y'rushalayim eloheinu sheheḥeyanu aveenu malkenu

LESSON 23

Student's Name ____________________ **Parent's Signature** ____________________

NEW WORD
מְזוּזָה
m'zuzah
mezuzah

NEW LETTER
ז *zayin "z"*

Now Read & Read Again

1 זֶה אָז עֹז פָּז בּוּז זָר

2 זָכֹר זְמַן אֹזֶן חָזָק חַזָן אָחַז

3 הַזָן זֶבַח זֹאת מַזָל זָקֵן זָהָב

4 יִזְכֹּר מָעוֹז זֵכֶר אֵיזֶה עֻזֵנוּ וְזַרְעוֹ

5 זִכָּרוֹן מִזְבֵּחַ מַחֲזוֹר מִזְמוֹר נֶעֱזָב זָוִית

6 זְכוּת מִזְרָח זְרוֹעַ מָזוֹן זַרְעָם עִזִּים

7 זַיִת הֶחֱזִיר זָקוּק הִזְנִיחַ חֲזַק וֶאֱמַץ

8 מְזוּזָה יוֹם הַזִּכָּרוֹן מַחֲזוֹר מַזָל טוֹב

BEYOND THE BOOK

Is It a ו or a ז?

New Hebrew readers sometimes have difficulty remembering which letter makes the "v" sound and which letter makes the "z" sound. Remind your child that the ז has a "zigzag" on top.

Jewish Home Treasure Hunt

A mezuzah is one of the many Jewish items that you may have in your home. With your child, go on a treasure hunt through your house and list the different objects that help make your home Jewish. Your list may include such items as Shabbat candlesticks, a Ḥanukkah menorah, a ḥallah board and cover, dreidels, a Kiddush cup, and a tzedakah box.

1 זֶה אָז עֹז פָּז בּוּז זָר

zeh az oz paz buz zar

2 זָכֹר זְמַן אֹזֶן חָזָק חַזָּן אָחַז

zachor z'man ozen ḥazak ḥazan aḥaz

3 הַזָּן זֶבַח זֹאת מַזָּל זָקֵן זָהָב

hazan zevaḥ zot mazal zaken zahav

4 יִזְכֹּר מָעוֹז זֵכֶר אֵיזֶה עֻזֵּנוּ וְזַרְעוֹ

yizkor ma'oz zecher eizeh uzenu v'zar'o

5 זִכָּרוֹן מִזְבֵּחַ מַחֲזוֹר מִזְמוֹר נֶעֱזָב זָוִית

zikaron mizbe'aḥ maḥazor mizmor ne'ezav zaveet

6 זְכוּת מִזְרָח זְרוֹעַ מָזוֹן זַרְעָם עִזִּים

z'chut mizraḥ z'ro'a mazon zar'am izeem

7 זַיִת הֶחֱזִיר זָקוּק הִזְנִיחַ חֲזַק וֶאֱמַץ

zayit heḥezeer zakuk hiznee'aḥ ḥazak ve'ematz

8 מְזוּזָה יוֹם הַזִּכָּרוֹן מַחֲזוֹר מַזָּל טוֹב

m'zuzah yom hazikaron maḥazor mazal tov

LESSON 24

Student's Name ____________________ **Parent's Signature** ____________________

NEW WORD
בָּרוּךְ
baruch
blessed, praised

NEW LETTER
ך final *chaf* "ch" as in "Bach"

Now Read & Read Again

1 בָּרוּךְ אִמֶּךָ שְׁמֵךְ עַמְּךָ דֶּרֶךְ עָלֶיךָ

2 מֶלֶךְ לִבֶּךָ רֵעֲךָ פֶּרֶךְ אֶרֶךְ לִבֵּךְ

3 כָּמוֹךָ צָרִיךְ הוֹלֵךְ אֵלֶיךָ אָבִיךָ עֻזֶּךָ

4 בָּרוּךְ בָּנֶיךָ עִמְּךָ בֵּיתֶךָ אוֹתְךָ כֻּלְּךָ

5 מְבֹרָךְ יִמְלֹךְ לְבָבְךָ יָדֶיךָ מְאֹדֶךָ חֻקֶּיךָ

6 לְפָנֶיךָ עֵינֶיךָ נַפְשְׁךָ מְצַוְּךָ סוֹמֵךְ מַלְאָךְ

7 מִצְווֹתֶיךָ קֻדָּשָׁתְךָ בִּשְׁלוֹמֶךָ אֱלֹהַיִךְ וַיְבָרֵךְ

8 תַּנַּךְ בָּרוּךְ וּבְלֶכְתְּךָ וּבְקוּמֶךָ וּבִשְׁעָרֶיךָ

BEYOND THE BOOK

Final Chaf

Your child has learned that there are five Hebrew letters that have a different form when they appear at the end of a word. When כ comes at the end of a word, it takes the form of a final *chaf* (ך). You will usually see a final *chaf* with the vowels ָ or ְ (ךְ ךָ).

Bending the Knees

Have you ever wondered why people praying often bend their knees and bow when reciting a prayer that begins with the word *baruch*? The Hebrew word for knee, *berech*, comes from the same root. There are two reasons for this custom of bending the knee, or bowing, when we pray. One is that we bend our knees before God as a sign of respect. The other is that by doing so, we are asking God to come down to us, thus making God more approachable.

1 בָּרוּךְ אִמְּךָ שְׁמֵךְ עַמְּךָ דֶּרֶךְ עָלֶיךָ

alecha derech amcha sh'mech imecha baruch

2 מֶלֶךְ לִבְּךָ רֵעֲךָ פֶּרֶךְ אֶרֶךְ לִבֵּךְ

libech erech perech re'acha libecha melech

3 כָּמוֹךָ צָרִיךְ הוֹלֵךְ אֵלֶיךָ אָבִיךָ עֻזֶּךָ

uzecha aveecha elecha holech tzareech kamocha

4 בָּרוּךְ בָּנֶיךָ עִמְּךָ בֵּיתֶךָ אוֹתְךָ כֻּלְּךָ

kulcha otcha beitecha imcha banecha baruch

5 מְבֹרָךְ יִמְלֹךְ לְבָבְךָ יָדֶיךָ מְאֹדֶךָ חֻקֶּיךָ

ḥukecha m'odecha yadecha l'vavcha yimloch m'vorach

6 לְפָנֶיךָ עֵינֶיךָ נַפְשְׁךָ מְצַוְּךָ סוֹמֵךְ מַלְאָךְ

mal'ach somech m'tzavcha nafsh'cha einecha l'fanecha

7 מִצְווֹתֶיךָ קְדֻשָּׁתְךָ בִּשְׁלוֹמֶךָ אֱלֹהַיִךְ וַיְבָרֵךְ

vay'varech elohayich bishlomecha k'dushat'cha mitzvotecha

8 תַּנַּךְ בָּרוּךְ וּבְלֶכְתְּךָ וּבְקוּמֶךָ וּבִשְׁעָרֶיךָ

u'vish'arecha u'v'kumecha u'v'lecht'cha baruch tanach

LESSON 25

Student's Name ____________________ **Parent's Signature** ____________________

NEW WORD
אָלֶף
alef
alef

NEW LETTER
ף final *fay* "f"

Now Read & Read Again

1 נוֹף הֲדַף חַף עָיֵף סַף חוֹף

2 חֹרֶף תֵּיכֶף עֹרֶף עָנָף כֶּסֶף שָׂרַף

3 שֶׁטֶף יוֹסֵף אָלֶף חָלַף כָּתֵף כָּפַף

4 מוּסָף צָפוּף קְלַף זוֹקֵף קוֹטֵף לָעוּף

5 אָסַף נִשְׂרַף שִׁטּוּף רָצוּף כָּנָף יָחֵף

6 עַפְעַף מְרַחֵף רוֹדֵף שָׁלוֹם זוֹקֵף כְּפוּפִים

7 מְצַפְצֵף לְהִתְאַסֵּף לֶאֱסֹף הֶחֱלִיף לְשַׁפְשֵׁף

8 אָלֶף בֵּית וְצִוָּנוּ לְהִתְעַטֵּף בַּצִּיצִית

BEYOND THE BOOK

Mazal Tov!

Your child has learned the entire *alef bet* and is now a Hebrew reader! Have a small party at home to celebrate *siyum hasefer* ("completing the book"). Perhaps you can bake a cake or cookies together and decorate them with Hebrew letters. Whether you bake or buy treats, be sure to celebrate with something sweet to show the sweetness of Jewish learning.

It is a custom to recite the Sheheḥeyanu blessing together when you reach such a milestone. Read the blessing below together.

בָּרוּךְ אַתָּה, יְיָ אֱלֹהֵינוּ, מֶלֶךְ הָעוֹלָם, שֶׁהֶחֱיָנוּ, וְקִיְּמָנוּ,
וְהִגִּיעָנוּ, לַזְּמַן הַזֶּה.

Baruch atah, Adonai Eloheinu, melech ha'olam, sheheḥeyanu, v'kiy'manu, v'higi'anu lazman hazeh.
Blessed are You, Adonai our God, Ruler of the universe, who has given us life, sustained us, and brought us to this season.

1 נוֹף הַדַּף חַף עָיֵף סַף חוֹף
ḥof saf ayef ḥaf hadaf nof

2 חֹרֶף תֵּיכֶף עֹרֶף עָנָף כֶּסֶף שָׂרָף
saraf kesef anaf oref teichef ḥoref

3 שֶׁטֶף יוֹסֵף אָלֶף חָלַף כָּתֵף כָּפַף
kafaf katef ḥalaf alef yosef shetef

4 מוּסָף צָפוּף קְלַף זוֹקֵף קוֹטֵף לָעוּף
la'uf kotef zokef k'laf tzafuf musaf

5 אָסַף נִשְׂרַף שִׁטּוּף רָצוּף כָּנָף יָחֵף
yaḥef kanaf ratzuf shituf nisraf asaf

6 עַפְעַף מְרַחֵף רוֹדֵף שָׁלוֹם זוֹקֵף כְּפוּפִים
k'fufeem zokef shalom rodef m'raḥef af'af

7 מְצַפְצֵף לְהִתְאַסֵּף לֶאֱסֹף הֶחֱלִיף לְשַׁפְשֵׁף
l'shafshef heḥeleef le'esof l'hit'asef m'tzaftzef

8 אָלֶף בֵּית וְצִוָּנוּ לְהִתְעַטֵּף בַּצִּיצִית
batzeetzeet l'hit'atef v'tzivanu beit alef

אָדָם	אַהֲבָה
אֱלֹהִים	אֵלִיָהוּ הַנָבִיא
אָלֶף	אָלֶף בֵּית
אָמֵן	אֱמֶת
אֲפִיקוֹמָן	אֲרוֹן הַקֹדֶשׁ
בַּר מִצְוָה	בָּרוּךְ
בְּרָכָה	בַּת

adam
the first human, man

ahavah
love

eloheem
God

eliyahu hanavee
Elijah the prophet

alef
alef

alef bet
alef bet

Amen
Amen

emet
truth

afeekoman
afikoman

aron hakodesh
the Holy Ark

bar mitzvah
bar mitzvah

baruch
praised, blessed

b'rachah
blessing

bat
daughter

בַּת מִצְוָה

הַבְדָלָה

הַגָדָה

הַמוֹצִיא

הַמוֹצִיא לֶחֶם

הַפְטָרָה

הָרַחֲמָן

הַתִקְוָה

וְאָהַבְתָּ

חַג שָׂמֵחַ

חַי

חַלָה

חָמֵץ

חֻמָשׁ

bat mitzvah
bat mitzvah

havdalah
havdalah, separation

hagadah
haggadah

hamotzee
blessing over bread

hamotzee leḥem
Who brings forth bread

haftarah
haftarah

haraḥaman
the Merciful One (God)

hatikvah
the Hope, national anthem of Israel

v'ahavta
and you shall love

ḥag same'aḥ
happy holiday

ḥai
live

ḥalah
ḥallah, braided bread

ḥametz
leavened food

ḥumash
Five Books of Moses

חֶסֶד	טַלִּית
יְהוּדִים	יוֹם טוֹב
יְצִיאַת מִצְרַיִם	יְרוּשָׁלַיִם
יִשְׂרָאֵל	כַּלָּה
כִּפָּה	לְחַיִּים
מְגִלָּה	מָגֵן דָּוִד
מְזוּזָה	מַזָּל טוֹב

ḥesed
kindness

taleet
tallit, prayer shawl

y'hudeem
Jews

yom tov
holiday, festival

y'tzee'at mitzrayim
Exodus from Egypt

y'rushalayim
Jerusalem

yisra'el
Israel

kalah
bride

kipah
kippah, skullcap

l'ḥayeem
to life

m'gilah
scroll

magen david
Shield of David, Jewish Star

m'zuzah
mezuzah

mazal tov
congratulations

מַחֲזוֹר מֶלֶךְ

מַלְכָּה מִנְיָן

מַצָּה מִצְוָה

מָשִׁיחַ מִשְׁפָּחָה

נָבִיא נֶפֶשׁ

נֵר תָּמִיד סִדּוּר

סֵדֶר סֵפֶר תּוֹרָה

maḥazor
maḥzor

melech
king, ruler

malkah
queen

minyan
minyan, ten Jewish adults

matzah
matzah

mitzvah
commandment

mashee'aḥ
Messiah

mishpaḥah
family

navee
prophet

nefesh
soul

ner tamid
eternal light

sidur
prayerbook

seder
seder

sefer torah
Torah scroll, Five Books of Moses

עִבְרִית	עֲלִיָה
עֵץ חַיִים	עֲשֶׂרֶת הַדִבְּרוֹת
פֶּסַח	צְדָקָה
צִיצִית	קַבָּלַת שַׁבָּת
קִדוּשׁ	קָדוֹשׁ
קַדִישׁ	רֹאשׁ הַשָׁנָה
שַׁבָּת	שַׁבָּת הַכַּלָה

ivreet
Hebrew

etz ḥayeem
tree of life

pesaḥ
Passover

tzeetzeet
fringes on tallit

kidush
Kiddush

kadeesh
Kaddish

shabat
Shabbat, rest

aliyah
aliyah, going up

aseret hadibrot
Ten Commandments

tz'dakah
tzedakah, justice

kabalat shabat
Welcoming Shabbat

kadosh
holy

rosh hashanah
Jewish New Year

shabat hakalah
the Sabbath Bride

שַׁבָּת הַמַּלְכָּה

שַׁבָּת שָׁלוֹם

שׁוֹפָר

שָׁלוֹם

שִׂמְחַת תּוֹרָה

שְׁמַע

שַׁמָּשׁ

שָׁנָה טוֹבָה

תּוֹרָה

תְּפִלָּה

shabat hamalkah
the Sabbath Queen

shofar
shofar, ram's horn

simḥat torah
Rejoicing of the Torah

shamash
helper

torah
Torah, teaching

shabat shalom
a peaceful Shabbat

shalom
hello, good-bye, peace

sh'ma
hear

shanah tovah
Happy New Year

t'filah
prayer